Sherry's Letters to God

There is always Light in the midst of Darkness!

7 Days of
Prayer
&
Praise

Author: Sherry S. Coley
Forward by: Mary H. Blake

There is always light in the midst of darkness

Dedication

Thank you God, for the gift of life.
Thank you for making me more than
a conqueror!
I dedicate this book to anyone who
has struggled with anything in life.
To those who has been tested and
tried, but still find strength to trust in
God.

There is always light in the midst of darkness

Foreword By:
Mary H. Blake

To the readers of this work:
I forward these letters that were written by my dear sister, Sherry Coley. I affirm, that they will bless and change your life forever. I am grateful that I was able to encourage her to publish these prayers in order to bless the lives of many!
The thing about life is that, it's not perfect, it's not a fairy tale, it's not all glitz and glamour. It's just called "Life". Life happens to us all! Troubles, Trials, Failures, Success, Disappointments, Upsets, Downfalls, Pain, Joy, Happiness, Heartaches, Sickness, and Sorrow.
As you keep living, these things will seem to find its way into each of our lives. There is a key to getting through this thing called "Life"! It's all in how you handle it. Simply because, life happens to us all. Many people will try to remember your past mistakes, holding you hostage to yesterday. But as long as God continues to grants us all His grace, we must keep our focus on Him and keep moving through life.

This brings me to why I wanted my sister to tell a portion of her testimony and how she managed life.

Sherry was born with the gift and ability to bounce back! I like to say this is a gift, because many people struggle in life, but some fail to get back up and keep moving forward. Whether getting up on broken or full pieces, her story helps us all to keep moving forward.

In addition to struggling to raise a family, Sherry had a very intense struggle with drug addiction. She struggled for many years, going in and out of recovery. It was the pain of seeing her children taken away, that would bring her addiction to an end. Her list of pain and struggles continue, but her trust in God, is what keeps her holding on. Today, she is still standing strong because she is a woman shaped by her struggles.

Her life has taken various twists, turns, and spins. Through all life's challenges, she has still managed to keep moving forward!

So, what is her secret? Is it her ability to talk her way through life? Perhaps her street smarts? Some may even say it is her ability to relate and connect to people, which becomes her motivation to keep standing. I like to think it's her ability to lean, trust and put her dependency in the only one who can help us handle life. Jesus, yes!! The man that provided the way to show us all how we, too, can be tested and tried, but still keep moving. Jesus Christ has been my sister's guiding light. She hasn't lived a perfect life, one without errors, or flaws but she has been constant in one thing. She always seems to find her way back to God. I pray these writings will help you too! Writing these prayer letters has always been a safe haven for her. She writes her prayers to God through letters and poems. Prayers for guidance, strength, and praise to our God. I pray that these letters bless your life.

Committed to Christ,

Mary H. Blake
Child of God, Pastor, Author, Wife, Mother, Daughter, Sister and Friend.

There is always light in the midst of darkness

Sherry's Letters to God

There is always Light in the midst of Darkness!

7 Days of Prayer & Praise

Author: Sherry S. Coley
Forward by: Mary H. Blake

Day 1

Prayer of Thankfulness

Dear God, as I come to you. It's me again. Your child.
God, today I come with a grateful heart. For you have done **<u>SO</u>** many things for me.
I am thankful for each and every day. I am thankful to be alive, to be able to say, Thank you Jesus!
Lord, as I look back over my life, and know that it hasn't been easy. I am honored that you have allowed me the ability to even be able to look back on all that I have endured and can give you praise.
Heavenly Father, I thank you for your blessings. You have blessed and highly favored my life, by Grace.
Lead me in the direction that you want my life to go and continue to have patience with me God, as I get better and closer to you.
Lord, I thank you for allowing me to speak over my life and situations.
Lord, as I learn to leave all of my cares on you. I thank you for always caring for me, helping me to stay strong and trust in you.

Lord, help me to speak positive today
and keep my thoughts on your word.
Today, I speak a peace of mind. I can do
all things through Christ that gives me
strength! I speak love in my heart as you
teach me to love myself and show love to
others. Lord, I pray for my children, that
they learn to trust you and to know that
you will bring all things to pass.
Help my children to know that there is
always light after darkness.
Lord help me to walk in your healing,
wholeness and forgiveness.
Lord, I know that it was you that
brought me out of so much darkness.
Today, you continually help me to see
light in you.
Thank you, Jesus, for being light in the
midst of my darkness.

Signed Your Child,
Sherry Coley

Reflections of Thanks

Thinking back on all that God has done in my life, in my greatest time of darkness, HE was there.
He was strengthening me and guiding me through it all. My soul gives God thanks and praise each time I can see my now, adult children living out their lives. It was at the height of my struggle with drug addiction, I had totally lost control of life and everything in it.
My life had spiraled out of control. My then, small children were taken out of my custody and placed with various family members. I know that the situation was bad for them, but it allowed me to hit my lowest and darkest moment. It made me take the necessary steps to get clean. It was the hardest thing I ever faced. It was the strength of God, prayers, and determination including the will to reunite with my children, that led me to get clean.
I knew that if I had any chance of getting my children back that I would need to work hard to put my life back on track. Many people told me that I could not do it, some even doubted that I would stay clean.

I went into a shelter for women, who also struggled with addiction. It was through this experience, that caused me to really see how bad things were. Together, we worked hard to keep each other uplifted and accountable to stay clean. Many of us, shared the same story of abuse. We made it our life's purpose to strive to stay clean and be the best we could.

I struggled many times after and fell a few, as well, but my God was always there to pick me up. He gave me strength to stand and be strong. I have been through many challenges, but through it all, I am blessed. It is when we face the hardest things in life and our greatest mistakes, they challenge us to trust in God.

Through prayer and determination anything is possible, if you only believe. The joy that I felt when God had blessed us to get our own home and stay under the same roof. God is Good! Nearly 20 years later, God you have kept me drug free! Thank you for covering my children. All seven have graduated from high school, some even completed college. Because of the grace of God on their lives, they have accomplished some wonderful things in life. Thank you for watching over me, as I struggled to come out of that strong addiction. Thank you for your love and strength. Thank you for keeping my mind. Thank you for never leaving my side and continuing to show me your grace. Thank you for allowing my children to stay together. Thank you for the friendship along the way that has made a difference in my life. Thank you, Lord, for this day, that I live in you. Help me continue to change to be more like you.

Lord, This too!

Lord, I give you thanks for your unconditional love. Your love is so much greater than anything I could ever ask for, or want.
I can recall a time in my life where I allowed myself to be vulnerable in love. In love, to a man that I was dating at a point in my life and had hopes to make it a lasting love, even marriage. He took my love, then trampled my heart, mistreated me and broke my heart. I thought that I could never recover, because the pain was so deep. When you give your heart to someone in hopes to last forever, you think it is finally the real thing. Only to wake up one day and see that the love that you thought you had, is now gone. Lord, you never failed me, you loved me back to life. Your love is greater than what any human could ever give. Thank you for allowing me to love myself. Thank you for healing my heart, taking away the sadness and loneliness. You replaced my pain with joy and peace.
Help me to live in your love.

Day 2

Prayer of Victory

Dear God, as I come to you, it's me again. Your child.
I realize that you have a plan for each of our lives. I let things and people come between us.
God, please forgive me of all past and present sins. I, Sherry Coley, (if you are reading this book, put your name in this place) want to be what you want me to be.
Lord, please help me to turn everything over to you. Please help me to let go of everything that is not for me. Lord, help me to take back control of my life.
Lord, as I look back over the pain of this past relationship. It makes me sad to know that I wasted so much time in believing in someone, that never wanted me in the first place.
Lord, I ask you to get rid of all soul ties that keep me bound.
Heavenly Father, clean my heart as I confess my sins to you. I was vulnerable and allowed myself to fall for the lies.
Lord, I am reaching out to take hold of your strength. I am looking to you for hope and a brighter future.

Lord, let me live in victory to live my life again in full, for you only!
Today, I speak victory over my life. I take back my life to become what you want for me. I walk in your peace of mind. Lord, I pray for everyone that is in a bad relationship that you give them the strength to move on and grow through it.
Lord, I pray for everyone that is dealing with the pain of rejection, help them to know that there is safety in your arms. Lord I know, you have brought me out of so much darkness. Today, you continually help me to see light in you. Thank you, Jesus, for being my light in darkness.

Signed Your Child,
Sherry Coley

Walks of Victory

Healing is all I can ask for right now!
As I look back over these prayer letters, I
wonder how it was that God brought me
through it. Writing has been my healing.
It allows me to escape my pain and go
into a hopeful place.
Thank you, Lord, for teaching me to self-
love. I now, know that the greatest love
is through you, Jesus Christ. I encourage
anyone that is reading this and has ever
struggled through a bad relationship.
You are worth more than that. Know
your worth, by seeing yourself as God
sees you. See that you are fearfully and
wonderfully made in Him.
I am reminded of these words that God
gave me one night while writing in my
journal. It was during my stay at the
women's shelter. I had to go there, just
to get away from an abusive
relationship. This made me never want
to depend upon another man, ever
again. I was told that I would never be
anything without him. I was told that
there was no way I could ever raise my
kids without his help. It took everything
in me to get out of that relationship.
I managed to live on my own ever since.
With each move in my life and every test

and storm, I strived to teach my children and others to trust in God, for all things are possible. Whatever you believe, you can achieve.

One day, I will live peacefully and totally free. I recognize that I am totally blessed, just to be free to live out my life's purpose in moving ahead. I hold my head up high and pass through the storm. Every day I bow my head to pray, he gives me strength for yet, another day.

In times of hurt and trouble, God take away the pain. No weapon formed against me shall ever prosper. God has my back without a doubt. He provides peace to all understanding. Whether I go through a test, or storm. I will ride it out and remember that I am truly blessed.

Victory Truths

My victory truths are:

> - I am a child of God in spite of what you see
> - I am Blessed
> - I am Beautiful
> - You called Me
> - I am Loved by God
> - I am Smart
> - I am Way too good to let someone else bring me down
> - I accept my Destiny
> - I am Healed
> - I am not my past mistakes
> -
> - I face my reality that I am Stronger than I think.
> - I am unique
> - I Believe in God
> - I Trust God's plan for me
> - I was created to win
> - I am victorious

Day 3

Prayer of Renewal

Dear God, as I come to you,
It's me again. Your child.
I am thankful that I can come boldly to
you.
My prayer today, Lord, is that you teach
us to forgive and forget those things that
beset us. Lord, these things are behind
us for a reason.
Lord, I look to you for renewal. Lord,
renew my mind to press forward and see
all that you have for me.
Lord with you, I know that I can make it
through every test and trial.
Lord, renew and recharge my spirit.
Lord, help me to see you in every battle
faced.
Grace and mercy are everlasting and
trouble never last!
Lord with your strength, I know that I
can overcome every obstacle set in my
path.
Grant me your wisdom to walk
according to your ways.
I, Sherry Coley (put your name here),
give you all glory and honor. Lord, your
name is worthy to be praised.

I thank you for the praise that flows
from my lips. May I always look to you
and give you the glory and honor.
Thank you for your peace that keeps me
daily.

Signed Your Child,
Sherry Coley

WOW Lessons and Blessings

- ❖ Anything negative can be turned into a positive
- ❖ No pain, No gain, No need to Explain!!
- ❖ If you believe it, you can Achieve it
- ❖ Do your best and pray about the rest
- ❖ Life hands you Lessons and Blessings
- ❖ It's mind over matter
- ❖ When you fall down get back up Taller
- ❖ Faith open doors that no one can close
- ❖ If you have prayed about it, then don't worry about it
- ❖ Sometime you have to go backward to move forward
- ❖ People can only do what you allow them to do
- ❖ Never stoop to anyone's level, make them rise to yours
- ❖ Know your own self-worth, you are specially made
- ❖ A good man's steps are ordered by the Lord
- ❖ Treat people as you want to be treated

- ❖ Never let anyone steal your joy
- ❖ Don't Stress, It's only a Test
- ❖ Positive thinking brings about possibilities
- ❖ Always do your best and remember that you are blessed

Day 4

Prayer of Hope

Dear God, as I come to you, It's me again. Your child.

God, I come to you to seek you for hope. Lord, let me rest in your guiding hand. Let your strength cover me as a shield.

Lord, as I reflect on the loss of my brother, it's been some time and years have passed.
The pain of him not being here still hurts me to this day, but I know that I can rest in your hope that he is in a better place.
Thank you, God, for the time we spent together on Earth. Thank you for the memories that we shared.

Thank you for the love, not lost.
Thank you for lending his life to us, to love, share and remember the happy times.

Lord, let your hope grant me strength to forever live in peace.

Lord, help me to stand on your word. I will not fear, nor be dismayed, for you are my God and in you will I trust. Thank you for the borrowed time that keeps us looking on.

You will always be missed.

In hope always!!

Signed Your Child,
Sherry Coley

When letting go is not forever

When people that are close to you leave
this world too soon. We gain strength in
knowing that they are gone, but never
forgotten.
Reflections allow us to keep close, to
remember our loved ones and the
impact they leave on our lives.
I am so blessed by God that he allowed
me to hold on to the precious memories
of my dear heavenly brother, Rob.
Rob, you meant the world to me. When
we lost you, so quickly, my world
stopped, because you were not in it.
You used to tell me all the time, when I
was facing my drug addiction to stay
strong and that I had the power to
overcome, change and turn things
around. You saw past my faults and
failures and loved me anyway.
Even though, we partied hard, we also
loved hard. I saw you become an
awesome father to your boys. I saw you
grow to be a hardworking man.
I saw how you always looked out for
mommy. You were the kind of man that
everyone wanted to know.
You kept the room light and always had
laughter to share.

I miss your smile, I miss your voice, I miss my brother so very much!
So, I will say good bye for now, but you will never be forgotten.
I will make sure to celebrate your life, instead of dredging your death.
I know if you were here you would be proud to see that I finally turned things around.
I'm still a work in progress, and have much work to do, but my hope will forever remain in God.
Love you my dear brother! Rest in Peace!

Day 5

Prayer of Healing

Dear God, as I come to you,
It's me again. Your child.
As I seek you today. I seek you for
healing.
Lord, I know that with you all things are
possible, to them that believe.
In all the things that I have gone
through, I know that this sickness will
also pass.
Lord, I look to you for healing and rest
for my weary soul.
Lord, I look to you and I rest in your
care. I pray for your redeeming blood to
cover my life and be a shield over me.
Lord, I release your healing hand to
cover my life.
Healing me from all sickness and
disease.
You are my rock and in you will I trust.
Your word says that you were wounded
for me and you took on ALL of my
sickness and by Your stripes I am
healed.
So, I stand on your word and I claim my
healing.
Your Blood has redeemed me and broke
the curse off of my life.

Sickness can't stay, brokenness can't stay, pain can't stay.
I belong to God and he will heal me as I trust in him.

In Your Care!!

Signed Your Child,
Sherry Coley

Jesus never Fails

God is my shield and in Him will I trust.
Even after my recovery from drugs, I
still struggled with drinking for many
years. The struggle has caused me some
harm to my body over the years.
Diabetes want to tell me that he will take
my life, but I believe God.
I know that if God allowed me to go
through my addiction and come out
healed and whole, he can do the same
things with sickness.
Sickness is not from God, so I destroy
the works of satan in my mind, body and
soul.
I pray daily for healing and deliverance.
My God is greater than any Sickness,
Trouble, Storm, Addiction, Pain, Heart
Ache.
God, has given us the ability to stand
and be overcomers in all things.
God, has great plans for my life, so I will
continue to trust in his will and lean to
him for his strength.
I shall live and not die, for I can do all
things through Christ that give me
strength.
I am living a victorious live through
Christ.
Jesus Never Fails!

Day 6

Prayer for Spiritual renewal

Dear God, as I come to you, It's me again. Your child.
Lord, my prayer today is to renew me spiritually. As I look back over my prayer letters, this one sticks out to me. It was my need to be become better and to be more like you!
On 1/8/2018, you gave me these words in prayer sitting in my prayer closet. I can only pray that this prayer will help you like it did me.
God says, "I am here, and I will NEVER leave you. As you follow my will, I need you to draw closer to me. You will have new beginnings in your life. I want to renew you spiritually. You must know that this too shall pass. Don't be dismayed for I am with you every step of the way. Today, I give you peace and know that in times of hurt, I will hold you close to me. Wipe your tears and trust that all things will work together for my good. I will renew your strength and make you more than a conqueror. I am giving you a new hope and you will live for me. You can begin again! Don't look at the mistakes you've made, but

see that my love for you will cover that too"!

Today, I am free from every stronghold. I am free from all of life solutions, and I learn to put my trust in you Lord. Help me Lord to be more like you.
I pray for a renewed mind, body and soul!

Signed Your Child,
Sherry Coley

Begin Again

Today God Says "Begin Again"

Begin again, he will finish what he
started.
Begin again, get back your Joy of Life
Expectancy and Confidence.
I will shift things in your favor. You will
become everything that I planned for
you.
I want you daughter to begin again!
It's not too late, for you to start again.
In fact, a new start on life will bring
hope for tomorrow, joy in your soul.
I just need you daughter to begin again.
I will give you beauty for ashes and joy
for your pain.
There is so much ahead of you, that your
past can't hold you.
Take a deep breath and begin again.

Day 7

Prayer for Spiritual Guidance

Dear God, as I come to you, It's me
again. Your child.
I come into agreement with your words,
that you will never leave me nor will you
ever forsake me!
In this prayer today, as I look back over
the paths that I have traveled in my
lifetime.
I am reminded of some of the choices
that I made. Some led me to a life of
destruction and others to pain and
heartaches.
I remember those places that I chose
that meant me no good.
Through it all, it was you Lord! Always
there to protect me and keep me
covered. I could have lost my mind and
my will to live. Your spirit has brought
me to this place and I am grateful that
you never took your hand off of me.
You allowed your Holy Spirt to guide me
through all my years of ups and downs.
You sent your angels to cover and
protect me, waiting for me to come to
you.
Daily, you watched over me and kept me
safe!

I thank you for having your way in my life.
I live today because you loved me!
I am here today because you never gave up on me!
When I was in trouble, I prayed to my heavenly Father.
You sent your angels to visit me and tell me that, I am loved.
You hold me close, and keep me safe in your arms.

In Your Care!!

Signed Your Child,
Sherry Coley

Angels All Around

Angels, watching over me Day & Night!

I believe God's promises when I pray,
that he will always make a way when
there is no way to be made!
As I look back over my life, I can see that
I have gone through many lessons. Some
to teach me to appreciate my blessings,
each and every day, some to make me
stronger, others to make me pray.
I now realize that it was God's hand that
has led me, thus far. There were many
situations, too many to write about,
many ups and many downs.
 There is one thing that I know for sure,
it was always God's angels watching over
me, seeing me through every fight.
Taking me through the storms and
showing me the light.
The other day I looked up in the sky and
saw God's angels, watching over me.
I looked up to the sky and couldn't deny.
The thought of it made me want to cry.
God is teaching me that things get better
by and by. I am so glad to know that it
was his original plan that he created me
to understand, that he has the whole
world in the palm of his hand.

Yes, he forgave and he saved, changing my heart in so many ways. He gave me a new start and created in me a new heart. I am not only thankful, but grateful for his love that comes from above. He set his angels to watch over me, leading and guiding me helping me to stand.

So, whatever you are going through, just remember that He has his hands on you! When you find you can't get up and you are so far weighted down, remember that there are Angels always around. You are never alone and you are never without, my God is good without a doubt.

The Night the Angels showed up

Angels are ever present, guiding me and guarding me.
On Sunday morning, I had just awakened from a long 7-day live-in elderly care case. I immediately heard a small voice say it's time to go home. I called the job to end my shift, they sent a Lyft driver to get me. As I was rushing to catch my Lyft driver, I felt an uneasiness come over me. The Lyft driver arrives, I get in the car and we pull off. He proceeds to tell me that his name is Aaron. Immediately, I felt a negative energy come over me, the atmosphere had shifted. The Lyft driver turned his vehicle away from the toll booth, that we were supposed to take. I knew from previous trips that we had to take the toll or EZ pass to get home. Fear gripped me, I started to feel sweat arise from my body. My nerves were starting to work on me. He started to drive very fast toward the opposite direction of the toll. I tried to speak and ask about his family. He replied, "don't' say anything". I'm thinking, OMG!!! He started chanting to himself, he looked up and almost did not look human. He put his hoodie over his head and turned up his music, and

began to rush down the highway, passing all of my exits that could lead me to Chester. Fear had gripped me; my phone was not working. All of a sudden, this feeling comes over me, it was as if the spirit of God was wrapping his arms around me. My heart stopped racing; I no longer felt the overwhelming since of fear. I heard a small voice speak" All is Well with You". I immediately knew what I had to do! I took my phone out. Yes, the same phone that was not working! I began to act as if I was having a conversation with my son. I began to tell him the description of the car, the license plate number and what my driver looked like. I felt the spirit of God raise up in me. I began to act as if I was talking to my son about God. I felt as if, there were angels with me. The angels of my gone family members. I said, yes God is good and he loves me. The lyft driver looked up at me and asked me if I pray? I said, Yes, I do pray and God loves me and my family. I told him that I had seven children and four grandchildren. I told him what type of work that I do, I explained that, I took care of the elderly and loved people. I then, asked him, do you pray? His whole demeanor changed. He took off his hoodie, turned down the music. We are still driving down the highway. All of a sudden, my voice shifted and a stern but kind voice came from it. I said, Hey Aaron, turn down this road, I know the way to Chester my family is straight ahead waiting on me. In the sky a distance away, I could see a beaming bright light ahead. I knew that it was my angels guiding me home. I looked up and saw a street sign "McDade Blvd" this was familiar to me; I knew where I was at. I continued to talk to him about how good God was to me. I told him how thankful I am to God for my life. I began to tell him, that God loves him too, no matter what he loves us all. He continued to drive straight ahead. As we got closer to my home. I began to get excited and I knew that God had allowed his angels to step in and take me home, safe. When I got near my neighborhood, I said stop the car and let me out here. When I stepped my feet on the ground, I got out and he drove away. I fell down to my knees and began to give my God the praise for bringing me home safe. Angels all around me, watching my every step. Thank you, Lord, for always leading me and guiding me, helping me to stay safe.

Remember that whatever, you go through, whatever you face. God is there to help you. He will never leave you nor will he forsake you. When we learn to trust God in every situation, he will always come through for us. Sometimes things will not work out the way we plan, but whatever it is, God will always help you through it. He releases his angels to lead and guide us along this path called life.

Day and night Angels watching over you all day long. Thank you Lord, for your ministering Angels watching over me Day & Night!!

Proverbs 3:5-6 NIV version
Trust in the Lord with all your heart and lean not on your own understanding; In all your ways submit to him and he will make your path straight.

To God Be the Glory!!
Lord, Continue to Bless my Family

In my Prayer Room!!!!!